# About

My name is Michael Lewis and I am from the north east of England. At the age of sixteen I was diagnosed with bipolar affective disorder. I have spent most of my life seeing my condition as a positive due to its effect of intense feeling, creative energy and a sense of enhanced personal confidence.

After my father was murdered in 2009 I wrote poetry as a way of healing and releasing the intense energy that came with the shock and bereavement. In the days before I settled down and started a family I enjoyed wandering alone to new places and spending the day busking.

These days I find nothing better than putting my family to bed and spending the night alone with an ale, writing poetry. Those three hours of solitude are my favourite of the day. That is when my thoughts come alive and I share them @peppered_leopard

This is a work of fiction. Names, characters, businesses, places, events and incidents are either the product of the author's imagination or used in a fictitious manner. Any resemblance to actual persons, living or dead, or actual events is purely coincidental.

# FOG

# Michael Lewis

---

## FOG

Vanguard Press

**VANGUARD PAPERBACK**

© Copyright 2023
**Michael Lewis**

The right of Michael Lewis to be identified as author of
this work has been asserted by them in accordance with the
Copyright, Designs and Patents Act 1988.

**All Rights Reserved**

No reproduction, copy or transmission of this publication
may be made without written permission.
No paragraph of this publication may be reproduced,
copied or transmitted save with the written permission of the
publisher, or in accordance with the provisions
of the Copyright Act 1956 (as amended).

Any person who commits any unauthorised act in relation to
this publication may be liable to criminal
prosecution and civil claims for damages.

A CIP catalogue record for this title is
available from the British Library.

ISBN 978 1 80016 301 0

*Vanguard Press is an imprint of*
*Pegasus Elliot Mackenzie Publishers Ltd.*
www.pegasuspublishers.com

First Published in 2023

**Vanguard Press**
**Sheraton House  Castle Park**
**Cambridge  England**

Printed & Bound in Great Britain

This book is dedicated to my mother,
Clare Elizabeth Frances Lewis

# Acknowledgements

Jamie Lewis
Lennon Jamie Lewis
Albessa Gonzalez Smith
Karolina Robinson
John Brooks
Jono Hinley
Andrew Paice
Craig Morton
Lyndsay Marie Duffy
Craig McGill

# Contents

The Painting Saints ............................................................. 13
The Crime of Living ............................................................ 14
Opulence ............................................................................. 15
The Slaughter ...................................................................... 16
Print ..................................................................................... 17
The City Walls .................................................................... 18
Walking Death .................................................................... 20
Psychosis ............................................................................. 22
Hinley III ............................................................................. 24
Blamed Ales ........................................................................ 25
Mother's Heaven ................................................................. 26
St Clements' Commentary .................................................. 27
Childlike Smiles .................................................................. 31
Snowy School Walk ............................................................ 33
Buried In Beer ..................................................................... 35
Lemon Haze ........................................................................ 37
Silent Rain ........................................................................... 41
Armageddon ........................................................................ 42
Red ....................................................................................... 43
The Roman Bath .................................................................. 45
PTSD .................................................................................... 46
Middlesbrough's Kitchen .................................................... 47
Attenborough ...................................................................... 49
Henry Bell ........................................................................... 50
Surrendered and Sold .......................................................... 51
Swinger ................................................................................ 52
Inquisition Begged .............................................................. 53
Blue ...................................................................................... 54
Crocodile ............................................................................. 55
Assertion .............................................................................. 56
Dylan .................................................................................... 57
Double Drinks ..................................................................... 58
Sirens ................................................................................... 59
Graft and No Go .................................................................. 60
Delivered Like Red Benn .................................................... 61
Wild Paths ........................................................................... 62

| | |
|---|---|
| Flogged | 63 |
| Entitled Tramp | 65 |
| Brass Castle | 66 |
| Lotharios | 67 |
| Spying Eye | 69 |
| Mystery | 70 |
| World War 2 Rubble | 71 |
| XY | 72 |
| Lewis | 73 |
| Faith | 74 |
| Destruction's Decision | 75 |
| Hypnotic Dusk | 76 |
| Providing Paradise for Mine | 77 |
| Fired Love Frenzy | 79 |
| Silent Company | 81 |
| Legacy | 83 |
| Butterfly | 84 |
| Burning Sincerity | 86 |
| Wehr | 87 |
| Planet Greed | 89 |
| Supervision | 90 |
| Mania | 91 |
| Heat | 93 |
| Bouncing Bubbles | 94 |
| Persuasion | 95 |
| Mermaid | 96 |
| Austerity | 97 |
| Strawberry | 98 |
| Reduction | 99 |
| Light Bats | 100 |
| Father's Pride | 101 |
| Winter | 102 |
| Lou | 103 |
| Dependency | 104 |
| Innocence | 105 |
| Hungry | 107 |
| Hollow Verse | 109 |
| Love Sincere | 110 |

Quick Sand ..................................................................... 111
Stretch ............................................................................ 112
Covid 19 ......................................................................... 113
Daddy Manic .................................................................. 114
The Human Horror Complex ......................................... 115
Paice ............................................................................... 116
Medium ........................................................................... 117
Loss as a Lure ................................................................. 118
Vincent ............................................................................ 119
Gloves ............................................................................. 120
Flock ............................................................................... 121
Dark Princess .................................................................. 122
Favour ............................................................................. 123
Manner ............................................................................ 124
Summer ........................................................................... 125
Spring .............................................................................. 126
Dreamer ........................................................................... 127
Fog ...................................................................................
............................................................................................ 128

# The Painting Saints

By now and by night the saints paint evening scarlet into
    the sky's scars
Flashing tango bars
Shooting spraying stars
The blue and auburn sign out
The silence begins to shout

The painting saints are striking song
And harmony with each brushstroke
The insomniac has slept too long
And now he types and tokes

The candle cries
Then hisses
Then dies
And now I can't remember

# The Crime of Living

It is as ever the grip that glues power to possession that pronounces my eye
It is I that glances kindly at anaesthetic tricks by the gallon
Each ache
Each anchor
Each baron
The holder of gold grime and the crime of living
The crime of life is sieved

Then folded
Then stacked
Then spread

It's headed high and without trying, it takes
It breaks when its stakes stay awake on cold nights
No child should be mild enough to fall by the community wildness
Each morning should be sworn to build the stye
Bye now, bye

I lied and lay in poverty
I'm unready to steady my stay in neglect

It never was

# Opulence

Brightness is before us as the sky asks the dark nights,
 'why ?'
Wet fields feel freedom as the heat peels
Bitter wind sings then signs out for playing days
When hay is rolled and bulbs rupture
When bays are controlled and tide is timid
As time lasts longer, we lay and love the ground
The morning hunger and chirp of the bird sound
Walk wastefully and sway staying
The night is patient and stars hatch like matches
From a borrowed thatched burrow we hold hands in
 harmony

The day
Let it stay
Let it live

# The Slaughter

The slaughter where the sauce splits
The cream cracks
Then curdles
Then crawls in opposite ways

The slaughter
The grip where the gun slips
Pointing its tip to the hungry heads
And the rich man pulls the trigger

The slaughter
The famine throws itself along the same burning path
That the good man walks barefoot, through soot in search of his birth home
Blazed and boiled in floating hot ashes

The slaughter
While the wealth is felt
Melted then stolen
Washed then wilfully shared unfairly

The slaughter

# Print

And now the leopard
The skin that feels sin
Looking like peeling pin
Mine

Blue sparks at midnight
Pour quietly then bury the chaotic day
So say in aid milk maid
Frenzy

Say steady unready make me love you
Force each eye by essence to try
Then sigh in dead love
Said love cry

Take each picture or pitch pitch-less
Chronic
Roll the hard part of my soul surrender
Upbeat take a seat and seldom applaud

Each chord
Each performance
Each sharpened tool let it rule

Sit
Dissolve into a stool

# The City Walls

For I've outdrank them and once again lonely I
Sigh and cry for a try at reduction
Sorry I say never
The wandering wild man may clench strength
From an elder ancestor or worse

Immerse

The dread that buries the soulless sense
The morning and what may it
Stay seduced by starvation without an answer

And the city walls
Well
The city calls

The city calls for an energy
A force
An unkown

A northern tramp that can barely bare a stamp
Willingly see and show the hard ramp
The steel mineral that made giants and brainless allies
Spies however
At the north or north east crease

You believe us senseless
You believe us dense

Can you trade deals of obligation?
A tough row in rows of violence
Silence
Rely
Spun span and thieved
We've crafted deals that forbid us career curse
A hearse for the under class
A laugh for the overs

This land is mine and with tongue and spine I'm coming
Humming
Plumbing gold and not grit

Sit and laugh
Sit and bathe in entitlement
But never fight as you've never known a need
A plead for your life

Knife

# Walking Death

Clouds are finally cast costless
The hostess waves and makes the deal
She shows a sharing care
But it's only ever dialogue

Beneath the rain, the huntsman hurls his herd
With word he struggles on
The load isn't layered, it is loud and heavy
It's full and it is worthless

His world is packed and pointless
A hundred weight it aches
With stakes he pulls his soul
The bets are beating the bear
And he bares his strength to weakness
He loads each cry with led and hope
The gravel growls at the ankle

Sinking
Sinking
Shoulder slim

The ground is bound and breaking calf
A half in time will quarter then die

Then smoke
Then smoke
Then smoke some more

A purple boil and mist like turmoil
A poison with each sin
Each sin to stop the heart
The heart is screaming for veins to answer
The opiate
The dancer

Like all chemicals prepared and dared
The habit hinders the life span
The caffeine fix
The female tricks
Abbreviated angst

Within each option all are calming
It's tobacco that says thanks

# Psychosis

The psychotic will often frame fallacy
But he always believes his thoughts
You ought to lend a hand or an ear
And perhaps call an emergency man

Sometimes it's best to never understand
And understand that you never will
Then bury the following act
As a debate lost is often a teaching

Be merciful with the tortured soul
And marry their muddled mind
To the warmth and heat of their heart
The pain in paranoia
A fraction to the reader
The debt is felt by the dealer
Not dealt but felt in lavish loads of layered lakes
Still never still the fluid forms
The trauma and the wish to wilt
The risk we stalk
To hear death talk
The promise to be taken

And bones we beg will be eaten away
By angels' aching stomachs
Then fly us high to yellow skies
To rouge where saints are silent

An hour in each nothingness
An hour of soundless fire
These are all of my desires
My family and a choir

# Hinley III

After the betrayal that begged him to sleep on his knees with sarcastic ease
The collection that whimpered into wilderness unspoken
The spares unshared that I promised I'd bury
In timeless rhyme and soundless sight

Blight
Begin

Without sin there goes the greatest creator I shared a shelter with
Sieve the start to the line
Roll on the spine where the fret meets peace
Never ceased
Forever the clever cry
Though whispered

Won't die

## Blamed Ales

The heart speaks its most sober
When boiled in blamed ales
My heart squeals its softest strike
As erosion shows the tap

Controlled conduction and clap
Belief production in laps
Soar the sour pouring plight
Rear rendition a roaring sight
Light
Like unknown
Blighted
Un-shown

The clever death that denies disaster
The slow claw that's calm and faster

Master
Master may I
May I sigh and sign a life complete

Repeat
Compete

# Mother's Heaven

There will be no nightmares or stares
There will be harmonious care and clearness
There'll be sights like bright binds
Where joy meets nothing

Another


And whoever
However or whatever you want will be waiting
In cleansed flesh and freshness

You'll see
Let it be

True to my word you will see
Trees
Birds
A third of rent bent then forgotten

Forever

# St Clements' Commentary

We're fools
We took each broken tool and stashed them, buffoon-like
A laugh
A good time
A sign that sang encore
Cleansed we found hope in each other
One another
Hope
Giggling grimy glares
A calm hiccup
A calm
A shout saturates and stalks without talking
Makes my mind kind
Makes my company though they're here queer and gay
Happy men
Happy tens of blind boys
Playing with toys that dissolve us
Evolve us not
Revolving and eclipsing
The strength remains everlasting
The morning clouds are casting
The fluff bleeds indeed
Wet
Wet

Wet cloth
Where moth meets deterioration
Stationed

# Pride

As for the north it's beaten
It retreated and dimmed in old spirits that shone sinful
Schooled as drool swills on pavement and across children's faces and fears
Every pier lay out along one another unconscious in comfort
A dead glow shows pain swerve from torment and torture to something un-rotated
Wine wails within rugs that hug floorboards forever
The ash is cashed and collected and each precious pet is neglected as it stashes faeces in carpet corners

The stench
The stench wrenches like trenches toll
The stench
The stench is a benchmark and as we grow ignorant we're shamed and showed

Communally blamed for big ideas of future and root rise
Size is selecting pride
We cried and we cried alone
No other but mother for shelter
No belt no violence no victim
Heat and clean sheets timely treats
Timely treats beat bruised cruises

Tell that to the many

The broken blind others that smother themselves in crowds
I'm very proud
I'm ever so proud

# Childlike Smiles

If it ends before I see your soul spark up with white light
If it ends before your eyes are surprised undisguised
> with blue clues
If it ends
If it ends before it lends me your childhood space faced
> in working class fortune
If it ends before seals wash up in the water
No slaughter
No sort
Nothing clinging or thwarting

Will you let me parade you around rusted playgrounds
> and hear you cry each time that you tried to collect
> a petal, then crushed it with many and dreamed of
> the world you would buy whilst selling your smell?

Which was built on innocence
And the scent of kindness was hell-bent on remaining in
> you as a woman
Though draining it stayed
It plays out daily
Daily it plays
Daily it stays


Morning you rush

Teatime you clap
Evening you wrap yourself warm and swarm yourself clumsy upon my broken body, like a rock worth keeping

# Snowy School Walk

Thrills ferment and force flattery towards thirsty tongues
Each gum is caressed and dressed by a smell of early essence
A stench stencilled into the brain's part that can only be understood by art
It starts when the eye asks why
It boils and brims with simplicity as the yolk explicitly begs for more early ecstasy
Chemistry crows and grows as a leaf is shaded on paper, then later it grows into image
Remember each morning like you forgot it then captured its sound with rounds of laughter
The brandy the candy floss
The sauce that simmers then pours as the moments adored
The cold I'm told is a passing pain that is whitewashed away by the rain
The fluff of the corn
The grab I am sworn
Is a moment which returns once in ten
Again please hang in as the landscape escapes you, it's calling to crawl back, it stalks
There's no surrender to seasons or dreams

I was told to walk in snow's footsteps
As there was the warmth and with pen I can show you
   the length of my mother's hippy hair
As she
Yes she
She was a breath of fresh steamy air
That frosted and glowed each dawn

# Buried In Beer

There in the depth of heat and heaven
I warmed into winter wilderness
Buried in low light and ink art
I'm sinking
I'm paddling passively as the water wakes me
Quiet souls are selective with where they taste their wasting world
Their tasting death and cess in unison
Their chasing agony with racing risk
It is always warm in the inn
It whisks the brisk bruise of rain
The wind is spun then men slip slowly
Glowing answers stare by sip
The hip is now bent and is soon to be spent
I'm falling
I'm drowning
I'm slipping
I'm warm
The grip of the booth boots me home
It's the lights I follow, it's the steeple
It's the heights, the horror, the people
It is now and it is too late

It is lazy to lay it on fate
It's not daisies or stories or great

It is me
It is hate

It is now

# Lemon Haze

I'm out the front smoking hand rolls because they kill
    me quick
Any progress on death is progress
Mother's in the back toking green
It's clean
She's smoking
She smokes

With raspberry dreadlocks of straight grey and brown
Not a plat but an impulse
She smokes

Lemons and raspberries
A strawberry craze
A phase
A sharp haze
She tokes

My youngest is settled in slumber
He's three stories high he's settled
He trebled his way conspicuously
He trebled his way three times
My youngest
My eldest
My middle man

My failed ginger glaze that's growing yellow

Like lemon haze she smokes

# The Bison

Do you see bubbles ricochet and rob you?
Do you lock them with a lid
Or a half?
Are you Northern?

Was your father Northern?
Do you believe in graft and grind and the guile of
 trickery
The spell of trickery and the lid?
Is your father Northern?
Is your father a wonderful man?
Was he always a wonderful man?
Was he welded by steel or was that my stomp?

What of your father?
What of me?
What of the peasant poet?
Is there a difference?

Tell
Spell
Then bury me south
Wrap me in carpet and count
Stain me
Claim me
Chase me

Have the nouse to accept each trap
Or beat them
As the bull blows and hisses in solitude
But the bull is often right
And the bull is often raged
The temperament of the buffalo is guided by girls
The buffalo begs for peace
He can't protect each elder
And he aches to wake in peace

After the deathly dive the bull blends and begs for balance
The bull has a thousand tricks
The bull is calm but licks his lips
The bull's breed belongs to the protection of women
Or a lady that lay spirit to his mother
Though she lives in black, she lives

But I am so scared
As
Is the bull

# Silent Rain

By the grace of God it is raining
The Lord has swung his sword and answered
The rogues are wrapped in trembling silence
The pyjama bottoms take shelter
The street and peace have chosen to meet
Laced in heaven's embers
Tepid, tapping guards are on duty
The smoke belongs to me
The humming hares are taking their time
They're sober and they're slow
The trees are fed and watered safely
The rats roam underground
Under orders
A perfect, sound new order

# Armageddon

I had a dream that the world was flooding
Thuds of panic in people
The final highest beating rainforest
Climbed in New York City
Suggesting that we may be doomed, I tried to cry the chapter
I'm a common man and common men don't seal the world to sink
I won the eye of four or five and tried to win some more
A duo of bureaucrats damned me not to drivel
I had five sharp and steel repeals
I struck three at the two
Then I showed the pair and stared a glare
The jewels fell in their eyes
I could have finished the earth that day
Some say yay
Some say nay
But I never
Never
Never did
I rose above the sky

# Red

Now mystery
Now pen
Write me and excite me
Strike the blunt ballpoint with sincerity
Destroy me
Gather me
Then destroy me destructively
You

Plan the play and play the candle lie
The thigh and each ask

The red
Red
Red wilt and forced smile
The bed let us die
Climb pain into me
I'll borrow strength and healing to seal it

A moment's death that takes nothing from free
Free
Freedom or force

Tell me of stories where pouring failures failed you
The beck or river or road
The duck that drowns immaculate
The rodent that keeps me safe

Today I killed a handful of flies
That isn't me so see I'm dying
A lake, a lust I'm floating full
The bull can't quell the rage but kicks for the red dye

The spread
The red
The dye
Grunt

# The Roman Bath

This is the Roman Bath
No romance bathed
We will soak in hell
Soak in hell
Forgive the druid that dares to peel us
Heal us
Feel a fraction of the hip end
The frame that looks game but is covered
Dressed quietly and curiously cast
No chastity
But bored with life

The strife of each brainless hour
The energy now pours jacuzzi-like
The whipped men and women show the spaded ace
The queen of hearts wears hers at cuff
Her majesty belongs to me
She is still by slumber
No number
Not by bedtime
Until the windowsill starts to gather gallery

An exhibition
No number
Slumber
Just her

# PTSD

Bicycle boils flesh and pours crystal through my veins
    to my fingertips
Grunting hills never asking for mercy but more
More agony
Tenacity tested
Tenacity ticked
Remind me I'm manly and more
More manner
Mustering malicious power and showering it trance-like
Bounce and dance

Strike

## Middlesbrough's Kitchen

The dwelling had begun to age
And the damp was starting to become prolific
The experienced villains were getting old
And the young tyrants hadn't earned it
The sauce was beginning to thin
And the steaks were breaking in height
The ghosts of the living stars are dimming
And the bores of the postured chores are starting

Once with warmth a chuckle and a shock
Once with wet words a cheek and a grunt
The counter stopped counting
The numbers meant numbers
Souls weren't striking and women weren't showing

Children, far many
Hence a shriek not a show
Hence a struggle not a snow in
No dancers just demanders
Hence a broken buckled balance

Never again and now chilled
The stale gaunt growth is growing
It leaps from the flesh of diesel
The gas is no longer gripping
The party is beaten by disease

Disease

# Attenborough

Demanding the sand and the sea to set the land free
The rocks and the blocks are quivering cold
Bricks and branches form sticks and rubble
Regarding the avalanches ask the cracked back of the wise
Surmise in size as who's not to lose
Nature's mother will rid us rotten
Heat in fluid will spore from the core
Preserving us as ash as it cashes us blasted
A frozen world is another wish of the earth
Ice in the numbers with chosen thunders
Rice and its shortage will starve the stomachs
Greed won't exist as crops won't amount
Seeds will produce nothing as trees will be freed
The chains that wrap the world's neighbours for the human's gains

Will and always will be wiped without thought or will

# Henry Bell

The pimp and the auctioneer are agreeing in price
The link and the production are thieved from rural centres
A sleeper
A slab
A sweeper
A slag

Now more than ever there's a guide and a demand
A hand in culture a foot in dirt
A brass
A claw
A class
A whore

The grapple is tapping the substance is queuing
The punters are sweating the city is burning
A club
A choir
A rub
A fire

## Surrendered and Sold

I have given in to what the bottle breeds
The cold quick freeze
The jiggly journey on every wake
Is a lake that right now
I can control

Will I struggle
Yes
Will I lose everything
It's written
I'm handing myself over
To the boozy belonging
The selfish state
The incoherence
To God

Cheers

# Swinger

I'm so low
Freedom five hours ago a fallacy
I'm so flat
Bubbling in breadth is bemused
Here I go
Wandering, wandering burnt
If only

Relief resists
A forgotten life
A sad face
A face that shows it all
An emotion uncontrolled

Begging today to be the penultimate
And tomorrow to be my favourite
Yesterday was obnoxious
The day before is dead
And happier days are hanging
The length and the depth of a swing

# Inquisition Begged

Words are beginning to look like failing me
But more so I'm maybe failing words
Queue
Clean
And chastised
If my life is loud
And I live for a length

Then I'll rot before I wilt a heart

Careless praise and not much added
Wayside compliments without a thought
But nobody wants to trade words
Good
Good
That's good

Has anybody got anything clever to say
A provoking inquisition
Words are failing me
People are failing my hopes

Once or twice please ask
Never

# Blue

We would be lost on one another
Stretched to the crevice of each other's worlds
Being nothing together in curls and webs
Things as they are may be clay
Forgive me in fields of will and wanting
Excuse me in elk with vivacious velvet
Pardon my plea upon feathers and fur

I never wanted to want you
I hate that I hold you at height
I'll never get to keep you

Blue

# Crocodile

Then this is what I became
A failed friend to myself
A year that passed
I spoke
And the words burned like butter
They shimmered
They landed
Landed where lust marries love
And love lies last
Breath
It buries the mystery
The more you pray the more you paralyse
The risk in retention is the hope you hold
Be one
Be true
Being here is fresh
The day will multiply
The week will wield
Years are blistered as yolk

Last

# Assertion

As the tongue cracks and the word breaks then in harmony the breath must execute
The posture still
The eye dead
The glare
That glare

Be still
Stillness is execution
Silence kills

Assertion

# Dylan

I've broken bones in the cells of imagination
And slogged at cess pit in poise of mercy
The day now as ever
Belongs to me alone
What have we got


We've got a time that's timed and wills to rush
We have time
We've got people in purpose that don't see it out
We have people
We've got grains that grind and grip at jealousy
We have jealousy


We've got love
We've got format
We have time in tides that pleads us to play

But nobody plays

Now

# Double Drinks

Does the drinker multiply his agony in rarity
Does the weekend binge come not often enough
Is there turmoil that's stashed and steams in staleness
Does the raging boy come out on pay eve

Then what of the other

The softer sipper who wished they knew less
That drinks with frequency and thoughts forget
That takes his time but begs for less of it
That strikes no being and gently dies
Is calm in clouds of candle and class
And simply
Quite complex
Yet easily living

Surrender

# Sirens

Why do I yearn for the fruit in foxes
And why can't I bite what is dressed and forbidden
Ask me again where my heart sits in slant
And when does a beat grip a gut in grimace
Growth
It won't go
Sirens
They won't stop
Stillness in persuasion
Heeled in hedonism
Lastly tell me the times that you tended
To try and die in a lie
Timing unfortunate
Trigger desired
Begging to be left alone in illusion
Bringing the brow to front of my froth
Timing trodden
Heeled
Help

Unjust

# Graft and No Go

Crazed caged an animal
You say start
You say stop
Jump

How high

The lion that screams for freedom
The wilderness with risk
The burning sun
And the chastity of chemicals

The idle breed and the feed for the nonchalant
The touch

The season for a soft pour

When

# Delivered Like Red Benn

Do you believe in freedom and powers and presence of life
And that work is a sin that the dead slaves indulge in
That the coffin the prayer and the hole that is measured
Should be passed as a burden and a worry to your kin
That the sun is a promise and the moon is a bonus
That soon unbecoming you will be ash and sleet
That family is granted and a token of treasure
That piece of gold that you hold can be rolled
That your back is a one off so you must break it when necessary
That time is priority that chance is joy
Do you believe in hope that the pope will grant you fair blessing
And the misery far falling will stretch out in hell
That the shells on the sand are handed from death
That purpose is fated or dated with grit

Do you believe in earth
The sea
The stars
And the burning

# Wild Paths

The thing that I need springs above all is adoration
Bite me
There's fragile hope that's forgotten in my heart
And it starts with sparks of lust
Tell me where it is
And show me wild paths
A staff and scarf with a blind purge and warrant
Just to say you care
In blind bravado I'll never dare
I'll never walk with a lantern
Dimmed in dwelling sold untold

Lost
Love frost
Costed a life

# Flogged

Worked
Ground into feathers that float
And chestnuts that flourish
Action is a necessity
Action is bold

I broke my cold back once
I stroke my held hold twice
I wait
Patience

You said it was duty
To cover wrists in gold
And your arms in ink
You sold me a crying scream

And from the altar I commented
Awake
Still here in brown robes
Still paying for what work owes

Not a thing
A single thing is precious
But harmony is granted
Ask and seek

You wanted to break your bones
Crush them
Borrow them
Then fire them up your nose

Cry

# Entitled Tramp

The worst ones are the ones that want
They're relentless
They have no calm
The strain and the stain they cut on your soul
They wrap at a passing that they never earned
They know better
But they don't know any better
And God willing they'll die

Scatter their dust in the grateful gesture
They did or they didn't know they were born

So be gone and go

And thank the lord there was a man left to say pardon

Not thank you

# Brass Castle

I'd love to pull a great big bright dwelling from some kind of earned success

An oak and brass front door with a knocker that belts in drama and dullness

An Irish wolfhound that protected me and mine and took care of its very own self

Laying by a crackling fire with me and shared the day's catch from a pot across a rug

And lastly a vast overgrown ground for my mother to plough and pick for herself with precision and patience

Then a vineyard with only red grapes and big chestnut barrels for fruit to ferment in wild red running proud wine

A love for wine family and the slow life

Not forgetting love

# Lotharios

I knew my way around women
The new way was dull
The drunken careless way was done without patience
A long time ago this worked
And lately when done correctly this worked for the majority of mine
Would I trade you worldly women
European girls that ask you for all of your strength in return for a mood swing and a meal
I never would
A voodoo woman with Caribbean colours
Who you
Or me
Perhaps
But again almost never


I want the wine to be washed against the wall
And the gold to grow in somebody else's gain
Jewel to be jealous
Give me the grateful girl
The fun girl
The lady that lays in timeless love
The girl that gives
The one that wants to be wild
And sing second

Give me the wild child that's cheap and loving
Make her blonde
Make her smile

# Spying Eye

Stricken at heart's main vein
A tunnel that blends and trends to borrow
Sized prized in sensuous slavery
Condemned to a gripped tip in rage
Aged it can only ferment in loving cement
A crush that won't pulp and when it is buried I'll say
    grace with haste
For now and for long my wild eye is spying
And I want to cut it out

Stamp it
Slash it
Burn it to ash

Scatter it away from my conscience and the guilt that
    grinds my mere mind

Mercy

# Mystery

My mind's eye meets at where we left
And I unconditionally wish that it never
In rarity there's peaks and eyes that join
And something left unsaid
To grow for somebody for a year and more
For those to keep it mysterious
Or maybe now and evermore my head has spun too far
The heart that's wrapped in barriers
The eye that tries to lie
The mane in all perfection
The lips that never pout
The tone that shows your strength
But most the class that asks for ignorance
And tries in shyness not to reveal
A speciality in loyalty and kindness
A rose that rose and was plucked
Tried and trampled and tread to touch

But what remains is beginning to colour

Pressed and preserved in perfection

# World War 2 Rubble

Men have let this town down and why
Died on battle fields
To breeding butchers
Unfed unsaid and unloved
The sour grape produced from rape
The singing sinning son and why

Why

# XY

The perception should always fall flat
And last
Lastly before I teach of treason
Reasons why my musk fell growth
Masculinity in lens must beg once more
To come last

Rage
Rage
And all things aged

Are begged to quill

In quaint disappointment where merely men

Muster
Merge
Manufacture

The happy home and the tree that swings

Men are bleeding

# Lewis

He barks and blazes in fresh frothed fuel
He glugs
He shouts and saturates a room in rebel
He's here
He owns an award wherever he wanders
He swags
Now or never he's tested and triumphs
He's ageing

If he calls you his friend you're in safe big mitts
Don't push
Invincibility is a fallacy
A freedom breed
Greed in grace

Immortal

# Faith

Pursuit of power was where holy humans began to sweep prayer as a promise
They asked and coincidence carried them un-clever
Forever and what came first we thought the unbelievers gambled
But it was us that rolled the dice
Sliced at pawns we merely met the Lord in fortunate frames and forgave him for the chance when he lay deaf
Mute we believed we were
The mind's final flounder was an ask of a razor
Given to the child that hadn't grown age
We trusted the books
We spoke to the last Samaritan
We fasted
Because it was easier to beg hunger
And starvation instead of looking at our sins in reflection's glass
The conscience remains
And the soul is asking
There's a word now and then we hold and pray for
Forgiveness

Are we vacant

Repentance

# Destruction's Decision

It will never ever end in flames
The people will climb the steeple and swing loose to heaven
The jugular juices will pour stored fat and fruit
The liver will be beaten and baked for the sake of a good time
The heart will break and the beat will take trauma to the next life with purpose
The hop and the ash will splash slash lash and burn then turn and take me
Not gently

It will never ever end in flames

# Hypnotic Dusk

Joy drips from solitude seemingly
Cars course the track hypnotic
Sleeping is for the dead
But as I'm alive I will yawn and scratch my head

There's a bliss brewed and tinned in treasure
A glass passed shimmers and shines
And the pouring amber softens the day
The black of the sip and the dark of the hop

Today has been far too simple
So the midnight's dimples must explain
With repeating lanes and pause of engines
Lights, they are surrendering
Dreams they start to ask
But the silent flask must be finished in peace
And the dialogue spewed out soundless

If I could tighten a screw into a heart
Then I'd do it daily and I would do it nocturnally
Now and ever breathes the shadow
It's looming
It's growing
And it is always gaining

Dusk

# Providing Paradise for Mine

I want the day's delicacy for my love
A harmony and a heat alongside
A landscape where only trees breathe
And an ocean backed by a mountain
I want the sun to rise without a rush
And green and auburn a promise
Pictures balanced on every flat
And music as a must
I want her evenings to prosper in calmness
A garden and land that is opulent
Food and fruit of the freshest offering
And company gathered by numbers
In sum I want the world for my love
And nothing less or missing
A fire that spits at silence
And chestnut stretched in space

# Living and Its Tests

The day has taken more than its share
I'm tired and the clouds have wet me through
I'd thrown my last so I turned to prayer
Every step that I take I stand in glue

My failings as ever are staring at me
The strength I need can't carry my head
There's an option that speaks but I can't see
My heart is sinking and my worries are sped

If there's a time in the future where silence is sound
And my mind can crown it without moving my limbs
Then nature's plea is to watch me ground
My soul and my test are boiled in rims

If life is a blessing and I find it misleading
The crisp of the sunrise and the sky when it bleeds
If courage is granted then I'm crushed with readings
Wrists are turning necks are swinging the new world pleads

## Fired Love Frenzy

Why do certain sales wear tails
Whilst certain purrs sport furs
Dots and spots for slotted curves
Piped in stripes for ripened bends
Trends lend a sending message

A colour is fuller and brightened by bust
Duller
Never so clever when red lips are pressed
Sex as ever is headed hips caressed

Boots trump suits and heels pump shoots
Nets in nest are ripped and ragged
Cats are caught
Bribed and taught
Shown and shocked
Grown then locked

In heaven all seven sins are binned
For a moment a sonnet a second a slide
Sliding
Riding
Hidden
Stuck

Roll and forget then bind in regret

Repeat until rhyming harmony

# Silent Company

I'd love to share my shattered shower of my melting muttering masked mind
With a character at candles' crown
When in grandiosity I'd love to lower preaching's teachings gatherings and grasp an attended attention without lapse
A builder be it
A joiner due
A milk maid many

But I'm always here in solitude
I'm sided by conscience and backed with brain
It's a tough love not to share
And a rough rant not to spare

There's a crumb in my head that may be dumb and dead
There's silence in the living
There's loudness in a desperate tongue
But the silent servers I envy
And they may want more of me

I'm accepted but I've fought for it
I'm loved but it has killed me
Infinite noise

The queues of quiet choirs never had to try
And the haters are still alive
They only needed themselves

# Legacy

This base begs to belong to motion
The tide turns and tries as ever
And I can't sit still in spirit
For now
And for a few more
I'm a whirl of wild wind and flowers
Petals prized and priced at zero
In return I have only one or two demands
Requests

Remember me
Wherever the body sows my soul
Remember me
Ask a question of me
However the acquisition falls in extremes
Ask

I'll meet more than my timeline's threshold
As for the first time I want to live
There's a common query and I want to scribble at it

Pass the pen and open your eyes

# Butterfly

Praise be to the soft shadow
The one that wickers and spits
The one that glows in peace
The throw that wraps like a fleece
The shadow bends and burns

It echoes and has no format

Glowing
Burning
Amber

The quick pour that takes its slow time
Time in mine bursts from thirst

The quick pour is time in mine

Presence is breath and as I breathe I claim
Thoughts of eternity and parallel paradise
Fitting in thoughts is paralysis
The quiet pour sores a fit

One day a steam train will regain its wisp
As this day is asking
Screamed for centuries and never sat for seconds
But a decade in time it inhales

And begs the candle light to replay the coal and the cold
That frozen froth was hours from heat
The winter walks when we knew less

Right now those golden chameleon leaves are floating
Like autumn in its surrender
The cot that cares nothing for the arts
The pram that pursues deafness and blind unkind demands

Tragedy

# Burning Sincerity

All that matters is the truth
Like fennel for flat fish
It can be dressed in humour
The agitation and aggression in deliverance
Or however else you make people laugh

The pouring woes of past promises
Broken
Betrayed
Derailed
Abundance of smiley lies
And pie crust confirmations

Fall last in vast hills of viciousness
As long as the lonely sincerity
Stands proud and beats its chest

# Wehr

On the day that the rain pains and cracks the craft of living
Alone in a field
With solitude for shelter
And dew for damp cradling
I planned to drink myself to the precipice
But retrieved a glimmer of grace
Space
It's cold and chaotic here
Heat
My love is somewhere warm


Guile and how I whipped my foes
Courage and crows that now surround me
There's a rug and a rough patch where the bay is beaten
And now I'm swimming silently
Bled butchered robbed and rolled
Sold
Priced by villains with less mercy than me
Hunted
Wounded
Won and lost

Yet the day has taken my final lung
Wrapped and spun in quilted carpet
Laid to rest and prayed by breast
Free falling in threes
Twice baked and sliced by snakes

Missed and forgiven

# Planet Greed

Grains are the plain purpose for starvation
One wants them all
Tall crops and many men to feed
Needed and span across four hungry herds
While more of us merge and mount our stomachs on crumbs
Slums and cess are best for the breast that can't fire
The choir collects and protects the righteous thieving sleeves
The mild of the crimes and the times that are piled
Have a question for me and a finger for you
Blue and breadline and living with hardship
Is where the lip of inquisition meets the mind of barbarity
It's disgraceful for gold to grow in one palm and be earned by another
The thigh tightens to make somebody's wealth
The ankle collapses to pay for your boot
Looted for the suited stray and the stranger's wager

Rebel

# Supervision

Forced to trance at a trend in a bent limb
Slim and stretched by binding black
Attacked and allured by netted noise
Boys and betrayal and guilty girth

Led

Leaded in layers of postured pace
Haste hacks and smacks in surrender
Pretender pressed but answers ache
Lakes of love with hearted heels

Wanting

Wanted wondered why, when, why,
When
Why

Sigh

# Mania

Life while mad was far more intense
An excuse for anything
And receipts for everything
The complexities of living
Meant a meal and an adventure
Time alone grew addictive
Swarms of enemies would stalk me
Rapists in capes worshipped at Stonehenge in a bid to
    protect immortality
Land could be tread turned and spun in volume
And all that gripped me was a repetitious rat bearing tail
    and teeth

When I was younger
Gums bled vessels of surveillance
Shaded lenses did a similar task
When asked
People would rush in a different direction
Contrary to calming my chaos
They would provoke my suspicion with proof
A man that lay dormant in a trench
With a sharp packed with daily drug and ritual

Screaming
Screaming
Screaming dreams

A brain that won't quiet
A limb that can't quill
A mind that asks and a heart that enquires

Torture

# Heat

What is left of life's cruel episode
The mind unkind and the brain's stains
A power
A higher
And a kingdom cursed

Watched in flicks of licks of louts
Shown in films of reels of heels
Forgiven
Nourished
And chosen by chaos

Scrapped then lapped at love's inquisition
Asked and masked in musk at dusk
Bleed he pleads
Slow she goes
Alive inspire at what comes last

And begin
At pin
At point
And go

Rattle

# Bouncing Bubbles

Pardon the cask and its bubbling warm breath
The crystal choir and the pipe that plays
Mellow at midnight
Mercy from melancholy
The wax skin sulks and parades in piles
A burden at best
Fizzing and frothing and lost in time
The monster marks out its mute mantle
What is left of the sin is sung in strength
Bleeding belief in a measured mask
Choir charade and a pull at pester
Forever in failing sailing slurps
Sleeping and sobbing and yellow yeast
Gripped and grinded by bouncing bubbles

Betrayed by habit

Betrayed

# Persuasion

Held in pelts of joy and ache
Spent and sprayed in lines of devotion
That holds
Held and condemned in time and rhyme
Release
Police my thoughts unlawful and provocative
Blend a blonde with red and rush it next
Perplexed
An oak blows smoke and ages life's pages
Read then bled in oceans of answers
Dancers
Spill parts of adoration sparsely and penned
Place cases of grace and forget that you met
Set
Saddled

Settled

# Mermaid

She's equipped with misery and the sum of sadness
Spewed in sighs and piles of pity
Hopeless is her glitter for life and luxury
The night time neared and she gnarled
Day
Dead
Drenched in depression and possession of prayer
A superstition stretched and fetched
More morbidity
More manners
Manufactured mildew more so
The mildest mingling of a tingling try
Too late too little
The day will only ever trespass

Blinking burning shimmers of shock
Worry and worthlessness
Multiplied with magic
Span by spokes

Old

# Austerity

Regular in introduction with pockets polite
Braid burns in time and tear tears of treasure
United we stand divided we die
Hunger
Helplessness
Heir

Flogged into frames of worry and pity
Found all alone in the starved part of town
We started together
You profit I tether

Regular

# Strawberry

I spied a tiny eye that talks
And blinks by blessed way
I tried to take its tiny hands
And fold in lavish lullabies

My welded sheltered curly world

I lied and grazed his ginger glaze
And rubbed his red rasps
I cried and crawled with carelessness
And sang and swore for the spring

My health
My halo
My hero
My home
My hope
My prayers

My welded sheltered curly world

# Reduction

The altered states are put together by chemicals
    corrosives and anything else that kills
Produced and primed at a good time and dined in
    webbed wonders
Turned tackle
Span sirens
High shyness
And anything else that spells sudden shock like hell's
    Inn
A shortcut to death in part
A begging for breath like art

In sum a deterioration of character and a curse

But a hearse by promise and pace

With space and sanctuary in stillness

# Light Bats

The past preys upon us with purpose and brutality
Currently in calm and kindness yesterday knocks
Chokes
And folds us

Easing into silence and shadow the bright light barks
Melodic silt strings bring stains then sting soundless
Shocked
And burn us

# Father's Pride

There isn't a thought or act that makes me prouder than
    the loud red locks that grace my child's mild crown
Everyday more beautiful
Evermore I beam
As the months perish I'm paused by ever-growing pride
There will be a day
A day we carve a cake
A week we half a holiday
By each and every passing second
I'm stale and shuck by his advance
I'm a love that is last
Let the years rust

# Winter

The grip-less gloss of the frost and the floating flow of the snow
Gritters spitters spreaders sledders
The rain splutters and gains in gutters
In morning in ice indoors in warmth
Outside the storm cried
At sea let it be
Fast forward last orders bring biscuits and tea
A stew is cued and Bovril is boiled
The sun begins running less haste more pace
And the damp is drawing with a frown on its face

Bring back the light
Bring back the heat

Bleak

# Lou

Wild spy plying the example from the truth
The calm from the fact
The day from the chaos
The wild spy screams and dreams of fiction

Jarred art parting motion from misery
Potion from poison
Glow from possession
The jarred art grasps for splashes of power

Culled bulls pulling paradise from slums
Carnival from salt
Melody from gun point
The culled bulls with raw rage wage war

# Dependency

I hope this beer buries me
As right now I want to hurt myself
Slice
Stud
Pin
Burn
A sharp to bring me close

I beg my ale to alter me
As right now I'm feeling pain
Smile
Pride
Sin
Turn
A love to want to die

# Innocence

A burnt out heart and a beaten lung
A choice of colours and a dark arc sailing
That's why clocks stand still
That's why clocks stand still

Stillness is exposure and feral ideas fuse
Slicing parts and a binding eye
That's why clocks stand still
That's why clocks stand still

Clocked in frames of favourite women
Twice they ask but one heart beats
That's why clocks stand still
That's why clocks stand still

Awake and beaten a bruising bark
A failing girth of want and warrant
That's why clocks stand still
That's why clocks stand still

And right there in gaze alone and buckled
A black silhouette that warps in form
And peers from shoulder to smile to application
That comforts that calms that cradles that can

Clock
Time
Bell
Ring
Twice
Beat
Beaten
Beat

# Hungry

Somebody was stupid enough to tell me you would
    climb the pearly gates this evening
More inexperience fitting
As you couldn't carry your greedy heavy carcass any
    further than to where you keep your safe
Many ounces of wealth are buried in your hands
You're dirty
Rotten
Hungry
Scum


You should be hung out to dry for raising a child that
    pollutes the poor
Carries themself in such a way
That destroys every opportunity granted to them
While we wait decades and starve to start our destiny
I only hope that there isn't an elevator to the Promised
    Land
And the hierophant doesn't take cash
Or the barrels of impendence coiled in credit

You married into muck
You praised a coin conditioned
Adjacent to you a life of smiles

But punishment pried in your eyes
And upturn turned you on

Profit poured in to your pocket
Deprived you denounced us

We smiled and laughed you never
We worked whilst you wanted
The catch was cut up in tenths
And you left us with a fraction

Dirt

# Hollow Verse

Lines upon lines above lines of trying
Bring about bright and debuted ideas
Layers upon layers above layers of lies
Bridge the breast to the brain in pain
Stains upon stains above stains of doubt
Marry the fact to the fallacy in frames
Drags upon drags above drags of grouting

Shouting

Between the thought and the expression

# Love Sincere

I used to believe in free love
I thought love had no cost
And I certainly wasn't paying

In human form it is bridged in trust
Birthed at connection
And blended by chemistry

For too long I stuck to the rules
Holy water and the choir
Now glory and grip and sips of seduction

Now love means more it costs much more
Doubled in price and trebled in feeling
Learn the last part later in life

Young

# Quick Sand

Quick sand
Quick sand
Quick sand
The world is showing its hand
I would run free if I was courageous
The days turn like stale pages
Pulling peers under
Suffocated thunder
The numbers are unknowing
The desperate pace is flowing

Quick sand hold my hand
I'm stuffed and choked and chosen
The busy lights are merciless
The cellar is always open

Slow sand, make it quick
Go stand and ache in sick
The pulling and the price
The culling and the slice

Quick sand take it all

# Stretch

Let me bring tomorrow to you as a gift
The morning colour and a string's shift
Let me show you the glow of each hour
The high noon and the frame of the flower

Let us stare at the sky as it ends
The evening and each of its blends
Let us grow and sow dreams to the moon
The night never burns out too soon

Finally focus on stars
The horizon is saturated like humming bars
Finally focus on peace
We've beaten another day that we leased

# Covid 19

For a full year this curse crept the worst from us
Turned us against one another and rehearsed a new age
But now the world is warming
Now the red
The orange
The amber and the yellow
The shades the cigarettes and the laughter
The stage the turns and the music
The times the wine and the wonders

Now the world is warming
The beating heat burns the curse

And now I see the end

# Daddy Manic

My nest needs me this night
To turn off and restart
As the cradle swings
The underwater swims
The life guard stays alert
The coast guard never comes
The hero lay awake
Dug in the depth of books
Heroine lay in parallel
Adjacent turning tongue
The eggs can hatch tomorrow
The branch borrows another quarter
The snorkel lends another
The guards are growing strength
The heroine inspects
Injecting tongue to a tumulus world

Wait

# The Human Horror Complex

Part with the thought as you ought to
Begin to inhale a fresh deafness
When your feelings bark
When your body is defeated
Noise and every multiple
A multiplying cry
Share your cares and affairs
Divided and descriptive
Over oral passing prescriptive
There is no way from the mind
So meet it with peaceful silence
It's the heart that drives the ambition
It's the brain that doubles the pain
Facing days can be infinite
Steal a minute for yourself
Wrap your hands in foil and wool
Tie your feet with sweeter pulls
And when you're ready for rest
Test the human horror complex
Next the unkind conscience
Vexed and prepped for violence

You

# Paice

Heroic by day with dark drifts
A gift
Climbing ice like spice in malonic mystery
My history
Immortal maybe as I'll try my time
Rhyme

Dragging life from strife without setting a price
Bragging never but blushing however
Pulling flesh from a trolley or car part like art
Lifting spirit with measure and balance and courage

Praised to children
Example set
A cautious bet

Paice

# Medium

All I ever was, was a vehicle
The world's worst energy entered me
The girth of earth's great glory poured

I cannot credit my thumbs
The transformer is imagination and numb

Blending flow
Bending and sowing
Form as a fraction
Denoted and juiced

Distillation

# Loss as a Lure

Grab
Grab
Grab and rub and weave with persuasion
Stroke stretch press and glide and slide as an illusion
Bury the bad in the forbidden
Bury the freedom in the evening
Plant power under the sun
Watch light rays bless joy beams
Strike suddenly with shock as an anchor
And loss as a lure
Strike suddenly with glory and heat
And class as a clasp

Never

# Vincent

For the voice to stop I must scream
With production spread across space
For the scream to stop I must whisper
With sincerity spelt by drama
For the whisper to work it must echo
With bounce that binds its truth
For the truth to ferment it must spoil
With fruit that's sweet and sour

Then the spoils and the fruit must be packed
Then offered
Then shared
Then packed once more

The remainder remains as a talisman
The remainder is the voice at the start

# Gloves

The vibrant act of pugilism is what warms my beaten stomach
The violence and thud of heavy handed men just seems to calm me
But maybe it relaxes my father's spirit inside me
He loved the fight and loved a chance
He was always prepared to die trying
Instead of growing old

# Flock

Every man picks his day
The clap of cowardice when he takes his own
Egotistical heights for the mild temperament
A handpicked army or a celebration
A chance a chant a belch
A grip a gloat a flutter
A splash a swill a couple

Now or never is misunderstood
Now not never
Never ever

Guilty

# Dark Princess

I am losing hope in this evening
And faith is further from my grasp
For the simple men are noisy
And the lady lacks her loyalty
Her kind and creed and colour
Is splashed and mixed with betrayal
Her time means trying track
And her followers drag her back
The hop that glides with darkness
The night that's dumb and deaf
If ever we were to advance
Would it cost a year of change
In order as there's none
Could we place a prayer for the weak
As the world is catching up
And the earth is unforgiving
The components from the day
Believing, as I then say
That family first and family matters
And family freedom flex

# Favour

I've often wondered if angels watch me
In sprit and in flesh
I've often wondered if the living, are mute
When they pray or push my foes
When the endless queue begins to snap
I'm curious of the break
For certain times I've stood alone
But I believe somebody has seen
A beam of power for good possession
Integrity internal and breathing streams
A weight that holds my head
Modesty
A modern bible
Skip the page and speak
The favour should be thanked and frozen
And thawed out on return

Pardon

# Manner

It rears right now to revolution
As it's easier than evolving
Why mind my manners and be a mild man
When rough is right in focus
The first time I spoke I spat
And swallowing saturates my strength
So now with power and drama
Single minded without worry for karma
Stuck to the thread and the pin
With swear words dragged out of the bin
It's now up to me to believe
It's now that I peel back my sleeve
The emptiness empties its rage
The rage then pours out on a page
Slack and stretched and folded
The limbs and the heat will embroil
And the tongue will bend with immunity
As to pardon a poet is theft

# Summer

Yellow warming
Orange bleeding
Red burning

Outdoors the clock saws as the times are racing joy
Wild cries the child tries to chase traffic never coy
We never tire for we are fuelled
Never eat as we can't be beat
Never sleep as it's too slow

Glow
Glow
Glow
And shine as the shadow takes its time
Climbing walls with seduction and slant
Birds are chirping bees are busy buzzing
Streets are joined by smiles and smoke
The meat then melts across a grill
The thrills from the window sill

Younger

# Spring

Rain I pray make up your mind
Unkind like rind you can't be stopped
Lopped like hedges wedge wood rack stores
Pours and soars of salty ground
Found in fields a crop from earth
Birth of bluebell and runny nose
Throws in field games for the ten minute drought

Daffodils, we are ready
Daisies, rock steady
Buttercup, kiss a girl
Buttercup, save my life

Relief

# Dreamer

Day dream carry me
Take me yonder to paradise and pull me through with optimism
Before it breaks let me sing sounds and float
Where everybody hears me, yet nobody sees
Fill my scene with colour and scent by peeling flowers fast
Opening their lives to share it with mortal me
When I'm done dancing sit me on a hammock and teach me to paint
Bring beer briskly to bury me
And raspberries rushed to root me
Let my liver last a long life
Let my kidneys carry on kicking
Quietly as the silent sound of life is my new love

On leaving show me the way to return as I yearn to venture virtuously
Pack the hour tight and prize it
And deal it day dream done

Pleasure

# Fog

Signs have always whined and struck to be looked at
People call it the gut
And folk call it instinct
In parallel the prize and size can be surprising
It's likely I that gets fooled
Schooled by reality
And taught by tyranny
The rattle of the pips below the hips are tokens spoken
    in dining houses where the stomachs are only lined
    and aroused with liquid gold
And seductive silver
Gold and silver are buried and splashed
Brass and copper in character when cashed
The day as ever belongs to the elite
But again this night is mine to destroy
The morning
What morning
The two hour plea just to register
The floating gloating grain that collects cloud
The glossy gain adds salt and sulphur
Then rains in rope and spares a step

Just enough to carry on
Fog